CW01431303

Alpaqa

JEEZUS!

Book by Sergio Antonio
Maggiolo

Music and Lyrics by
Sergio Antonio Maggiolo and
Guido García Lueches

Created with Laura Killeen

concord
theatricals

FOR AMATEUR PRODUCTION ENQUIRIES

UNITED KINGDOM AND WORLD
EXCLUDING NORTH AMERICA
licensing@concordtheatricals.co.uk

020-7054-7298

Each title is subject to availability from Concord Theatricals,
depending upon country of performance.

USE OF COPYRIGHTED MUSIC

USE OF COPYRIGHTED THIRD-PARTY MATERIALS

IMPORTANT BILLING AND CREDIT REQUIREMENTS

NOTE

This edition reflects a rehearsal draft of the script and may differ from the final production.

JEEZUS! was first developed by Alpaqa at Camden People's Theatre in London in March 2023, The Pleasance in April 2024, and Brixton House in October 2024. The team went on to win the Edinburgh Untapped award to further develop the play for the Edinburgh Fringe. The musical premiered at Underbelly at the Edinburgh Fringe on 31 July 2025, produced by New Diorama Theatre. The cast and creative team were as follows:

MIGUEL/JESÚS .... Sergio Antonio Maggiolo
GABRIEL/JOSÉ/MARÍA
FATHER ANGELO/JEEZUS .... Guido García Luechess

BOOK................................... Sergio Antonio Maggiolo
MUSIC & LYRICS .... Sergio Antonio Maggiolo
                                       & Guido García Lueches
DIRECTOR & CO-CREATOR .... Laura Killeen
PRODUCER .... Terraza Producciones
COSTUME & PROPS DESIGNER.................. Carolina Rieckhof
CHOREOGRAPHER .... Vivian Gabel
MUSICAL SUPERVISOR & ORCHESTRATOR ....Tom Cagnoni
DRAMATURG .... Alejandro Clavier

UNTAPPED

UNDERBELLY | NEW DIORAMA THEATRE | CONCORD THEATRICALS

Originally developed in 2018 by New Diorama and Underbelly to discover and support emerging theatre makers at the Edinburgh Festival Fringe, the Untapped Award has established a remarkable record as a platform for bold new theatre by outstanding companies.

Over the last seven years, the Untapped Award has provided a springboard for a diverse array of major Edinburgh Fringe premieres. Previous recipients have gone on to win three Fringe First Awards – *This is Not a Show About Hong Kong* (Max Percy & Friends); *It's True, It's True, It's True* (Breach); *Dressed* (ThisEgg) – and *The Stage* Edinburgh Award – *Queens of Sheba* (Nouveau Riche). Winners have also gone on to secure major national and international tours following the festival, including Side Eye Productions' *Dugsi Dayz* (Royal Court transfer), FlawBored's *It's A Motherf**king Pleasure* (*The Stage*'s The Fringe Five), Burnt Lemon's *Tokyo Rose*, Ugly Bucket's *Good Grief* and Nouveau Riche's *Queens of Sheba*, which most recently played at New York's Public Theater for the prestigious Under the Radar Festival, and adaptations for screen, with *It's True, It's True, It's True* broadcast on BBC television.

"The Untapped trio ranked among the best of the entire festival, proof that support from organisations like Underbelly and New Diorama can pay off in spades." – *WhatsOnStage*

In 2023, the award was relaunched and super-charged with support from new partners Concord Theatricals, with the cash investment in each company doubled to £10,000 alongside an extensive paid-for support package and publication by Concord Theatricals under their UK imprint Samuel French Ltd.

Drawn from a nationwide talent search, the three 2025 winners are *Ways of Knowing* by Emergency Chorus, a mysterious and slippery dance-theatre work exploring the impossibility of predicting the future; *JEEZUS!* by Alpaqa, a bold, irreverent, and euphoric South American musical comedy celebrating self-discovery, faith, and queerness; and *Pigs Fly Easy Ryan* by NONSTOP, an aviation bimbofication transubstantiation ritual following two flamin' hot flight fetishists as they sneaky-weaky their way to freedom.

New Diorama Theatre

New Diorama Theatre is a pioneering studio venue in the heart of London.

Based on the corner of Regent's Park, over the last fifteen years New Diorama has been at the heart of a new movement in British theatre. New Diorama is the only venue in the UK entirely dedicated to providing a home for the country's best independent theatre companies and ensembles, and has established a national record as a trailblazer for early-career artist support.

"A genuine theatrical phenomenon – a miniature powerhouse." – *The Stage*

In 2022, New Diorama was named *The Stage*'s Fringe Theatre Of The Year for the second time in its short history, and in 2023 was awarded the inaugural Critics Circle Empty Space Venue Award. Since opening in 2010, New Diorama's work has also won four prestigious Peter Brook Awards, eleven Off West End Awards including Off West End Artistic Director of the Year, and The Stage's Innovation Prize.

"A must-visit destination for London theatregoers." – *Time Out*

Work commissioned and produced at New Diorama frequently tours nationally and internationally, including regular transfers Off-Broadway and co-curating New York's celebrated Brits Off Broadway Festival with 59E59 Theaters. The Stage 100, which charts power and influence across British Theatre, currently list New Diorama as the most influential independent studio theatre in the UK.

"A crucial part of the wider UK theatre ecology and an under-sung hero." – *The Guardian*

In 2023, New Diorama achieved a further milestone with two original commissions transferring into London's West End. *For Black Boys Who Have Considered Suicide When The Hue Gets Too Heavy*, originally co-produced with Nouveau Riche and earning their artistic director Ryan Calais-Cameron an Olivier Award nomination for Best New Play, transferred first to the Royal Court Theatre before sell-out West End runs at the Apollo Theatre and Garrick Theatre. Alongside, *Operation Mincemeat*, an original New Diorama commission from musical theatre company SpitLip, won the 2024 Olivier Award for Best New Musical and is currently running at the Fortune Theatre on the West End, across the country on its first national tour, and at the Golden Theatre on Broadway, where it won the 2025 Tony Award for Best Performance by a Featured Actor in a Musical.

"New Diorama has only been around for a decade but has already left a huge mark on the global theatre scene." – *WhatsOnStage*

www.newdiorama.com | @NewDiorama | New Diorama Theatre, 15-16 Triton Street, Regent's Place, London NW1 3BF.

Head of Programme....................................Emma Clark

Head of Communications ....Flavia Fraser-Cannon

Artist Support Producer ....Stella Green

Executive Director & Co-CEO ....Jonathan Maydew-Gale

General Manager .... Ryan Mellish

Finance Director..Jo Salkilld

Production Manager.................................... Sy Supersad

Executive Producer & Co-CEO........................Sophie Wallis

Café & Bar Manager....................................Will Watson

CYT Facilitators ....Phoebe Fairchild, Shamira Turner

CYT Producer .... Regina Agard-Brathwaite

Trainee CYT Facilitator ....Rhys Howarth

Front of House & Café Team .... Eileen Amina, Alexandru Bot, Beth Organ, Cameron Tebira, Rhys Howarth, Teddy Robinson, Laurie Ward

underbelly

Established in 2000, Underbelly is a UK-based live entertainment company specialising in programming and producing ground-breaking theatrical productions, cultural city centre events and original festivals.

Founded at the Edinburgh Festival Fringe by Ed Bartlam and Charlie Wood, Underbelly remains a pioneer of untapped talent across the world of theatre, comedy, circus and cabaret, entertaining audiences from London to Edinburgh, and Asia to North America.

As a leading venue producer at the Edinburgh Festival Fringe, Underbelly's 2025 programme will welcome over 160+ shows across 20 performances spaces. 2025 marks Underbelly's 25th year at the festival, celebrating a wealth of programming highlights from across the years including Phoebe Waller-Bridge's *Fleabag* in 2013, Marlow and Moss' *SIX* in 2018, Manual Cinema's *Ada/Ava* in 2016, 1927's *Between the Devil and the Deep Blue Sea* in 2007, Rob Madge's *My Son's A Queer (But What Can You Do?)* in 2022 and Francesca Moody Productions' *Kathy & Stella Solve a Murder!* in 2023.

On the West End, Underbelly is the lead and originating producer of the Olivier Award-winning revival of *Cabaret* at the Kit Kat Club, alongside ATG Productions, now in its fourth year and originally starring Eddie Redmayne and Jessie Buckley.

Since 2023 Underbelly has also been welcoming audiences to its first permanent venue, Underbelly Boulevard Soho, in the heart of London. A vibrant and dynamic entertainment destination boasting a state-of-the-art auditorium, Underbelly Boulevard Soho plays host to world-class cabaret, comedy, theatre and circus year-round; with previous residencies including Steven Frayne's *Up Close and Magical*; Bernie Dieter's *Club Kabarett*; Three Legged Race Productions' *Sophie's Surprise 29th*; Flo & Joan's *One Man Musical*; John Bishop; Josh Thomas; Tim Key; and Mario The Maker Magician.

In 2025 Underbelly has partnered with the Nevill Holt Festival in the heart of the Leicestershire countryside. Building on a decade of opera performances, the festival now includes opera, concerts, conversations, performances, art exhibitions, family events and open gardens. The 2025 programme features performances from the likes of Jalen Ngonda and Ronnie Scott's Jazz Orchestra; talks from National treasures such as Richard E. Grant and Prue Leith; as well as signalling the start of a five-year partnership with Opera North as they bring to life Mozart's *Così fan tutte*.

Other recent credits include *Macbeth* starring Ralph Fiennes and Indira Varma in partnership with Wessex Grove (UK Tour), The McOnie Company's *Nutcracker* at the Tuff Nutt Jazz Club (Southbank Centre), *Tweedy's Massive Circus* (UK Tour), *Five Guys Named Moe* (Marble Arch Theatre) Oliver Award-nominated for Best Entertainment; *Cabaret Royale* (Gaillard Centre, Charleston USA); and *La Clique* (London, Edinburgh, Manchester and Singapore).

www.underbelly.co.uk | @FollowTheCow | @underbellyedinburgh | @underbellyent

Directors............................ Ed Bartlam and Charlie Wood
PA to Directors and Office Manager .... Lauren Manning

Head of Programming and Producer .... Marina Dixon
Senior Programmer .... Jodie Adams
Senior Producer..................................... Áine Flanagan
Festival Programmer .... Alex Cofield
Programming Administrator .... Frankie Arnold

Head of Marketing .... Lauren Carroll
Marketing Manager .... Hope Martin
Marketing Officer .... Beth Toeman

Head of Production.................................... Ian Gibbs
Senior Production Manager .... Kenny Easson
Warehouse and Logistics Manager .... Steven Kilpatrick

Senior Event Producer................................ Ruth Fisher
Senior Event Producer........................ Rachel Sivills-McCann

Head of Operations.................................. Ryan Beattie
Operations Manager..................................... Joe Mills

Head of Ticketing .... Natalie Norman
Box Office and Customer Service Manager .... James Farmer
Head of Food & Beverage............................. Steve Clarke
Head of Brand Partnerships .... Mary Gleeson
Head of Finance .... Jenny Glanville

ALPAQA

ALPAQA is the collaborative efforts of Sergio Antonio Maggiolo, Laura Killeen & Guido García Lueches. They create work about urgent political topics, whilst at the same time being as silly as possible. Their work has been celebrated for its boldness, humour, and emotional depth, receiving strong audience reactions: Laughter, tears, standing ovations and heartfelt engagement. Laura and Sergio have a long history of collaboration, particularly in their long-running show *The Dirty Thirty* (Rosemary Branch, VAULT Festival & others, since 2017), where they regularly write and present short non-fictional plays with the London Neo-Futurists.

Sergio and Guido have been real-life partners since 2020, and frequently collaborate in each other's projects, including *Un Intento Valiente* (Spain), *Playing Latinx* (Summerhall 2023, Soho Theatre 2024), *...Earnest?* (by *Say it Again, Sorry?*, EdFringe & UK Tour).

Guido & Laura previously worked together on *Distant Memories of the Near Future* (Summerhall 2023, Arcola 2024). This is their first full length show working together.

TERRAZA PRODUCCIONES

TERRAZA PRODUCCIONES is a newly established theatre production company founded by Guido García Lueches and Sergio Antonio Maggiolo. They develop and produce bold, queer, Latinx-led performance that is intimate, irreverent, and energetically camp. Their work blends political urgency with humour, music, and lived experience, often blurring the line between autobiography and absurdity.

The name TERRAZA honors both the plastic patio chairs of Latin America, those iconic seats of chisme, revolution, and everyday ritual, and the first address we ever shared. It is where we began building a life together, and now, a company. For us, a terraza is not just a place. It is a point of view: informal, open to the street, and full of potential.

Our debut project is *JEEZUS!*, a queer musical created and performed by Sergio and Guido, winner of the 2025 Untapped Award and premiering at the Edinburgh Fringe.

We make work that sits where laughter meets rebellion.

THE
ROSEMARY
BRANCH
THEATRE · PUB · KITCHEN

The Rosemary Branch Theatre, affectionately known as the Rosie, is an award-winning independent venue on the border of Islington and Hackney, London. Nestled above a historic pub, the Rosie has been a space of entertainment for centuries, whether pleasure gardens, music hall, or comedy, music and theatre venue. Having fallen into disrepair in the early 1990s, it began life again as a vibrant cultural hub in 1996, when it was resurrected by Cecilia Darker, Cleo Sylvestre and Angela Neustatter. Angela stepped away after a short time, leaving Cec and Cleo to run the Theatre for almost 20 years. Under their stewardship, the Theatre became known for offering a diverse range of performance, as well as being a welcoming space for experienced theatre makers and new artists alike.

Former intern Scarlett Plouviez Comnas continued their ethos and added her own innovative stamp from 2016-2020, running the Theatre alongside Genevieve Taricco.

Since 2021 the Rosemary Branch has been under the leadership of Artistic Director Laura Killeen. During this time the theatre's programming has continued to build on its founders' legacies and values, developing new writing – like Haley McGee's *Age Is A Feeling* - and supporting artists of the global majority – like Saher Shah's award winning *Vitamin D*. Three annual festivals have been established to support new work; the Curious Puppets puppetry festival, Look For The Woman Festival of female and femme comedy and clowning, and Gather Together Storytelling Festival. With its intimate 60-seat auditorium, the Rosemary Branch has cultivated a reputation for nurturing emerging talent while providing a welcoming space for established artists to showcase their work.

As a proud champion of creativity and inclusivity, the Rosemary Branch Theatre is committed to fostering community engagement through its eclectic programming and outreach initiatives. It is a historic space with a modern outlook, and has been female-led for 29 years. Its strong ties to London's artistic scene have made it a beloved institution, contributing to its vibrant and ever-growing legacy.

Artistic Director | Laura Killeen

Technical Director | Helen Potter

With grateful thanks to our wonderful Front of House team.

CAST

SERGIO ANTONIO MAGGIOLO | Miguel and Jesús / Book & Lyrics

Sergio Maggiolo is a queer, London-based writer, performer, and director born in Peru and trained in the U.S. Known for making theatre that is political, irreverent, and charged with emotional truth, Sergio's work blends personal experience with collective memory, often through playful, genre-defying forms. They began their career onscreen in Peruvian television before training at NYU's Atlantic Acting School and ultimately settling in the UK, where they've built a career across stages in Europe, Latin America, and Asia.

Sergio has directed and performed in acclaimed productions at venues including Brixton House, The Arcola, Southwark Playhouse, The Pleasance, and Teatro Alfil Madrid. They are a founding member of *Un Intento Valiente*, a neofuturist performance collective, and a core artist with Degenerate Fox.

This is their debut publication – a text that, like all their work, speaks from the body and toward a better future.

GUIDO GARCÍA LUECHES | Gabriel and Others / Music & Lyrics

Guido is a Uruguayan actor, poet and theatre maker, working in the UK since 2015. They trained at the Instituto de Actuación de Montevideo, Uruguay and Associated Studios, London. They co-founded interactive theatre company Say It Again, Sorry? with whom they created the hit interactive comedy *...Earnest?* now on a UK tour. Guido's first solo show *Playing Latinx* played the Edinburgh Fringe 2023 to rave reviews, and later transferred to Soho Theatre.

Other UK performing credits include: *The Highwayman* (Norwich Theatre & tour), *A Midsummer Night's Dream* (Roman Theatre St Alban's) , *The Winter's Tale* (Minack Theatre), *NewsRevue* (Canal Cafe), *Les Liaisons Dangereuses* (OVO), *The Jungle Book* (Watermill Theatre), *It Happened in Key West* (Charing Cross Theatre), *The Boy Who Cried Wolf* (York Theatre Royal / Tutti Frutti).

CREATIVE

LAURA KILLEEN | Director & Co-creator

Laura Killeen is a director and theatre maker from London. Directing credits include *JEEZUS!* (Edinburgh Untapped Award 2025 Winner, New Diorama Theatre, Brixton House), *Godot Is A Woman* (Pleasance, Cambridge Junction, King's Head Theatre, UK Tour), Distant Memories of the Near Future (Arcola, Summerhall), *Hold the Line* (7from 7 Winner, 7 Dials Playhouse) and *Chopped Liver & Unions* (59E59 New York - Brits Off Broadway). Her directing work has garnered 4 and 5 star reviews from publications including *The Guardian, The Stage, The Scotsman* and *Broadway World.*

Laura regularly works with playwrights, solo performers, stand-up comedians and theatre companies as a dramaturg. A published writer, her work has been performed in Asia, Europe and North & South America. She has performed in numerous plays on both sides of the pond, as well as award winning film, radio, and performance art. laurakilleen.com

CAROLINA RIECKHOF | Costume & Props Designer

Carolina Rieckhof holds an MA in Costume Design for Performance and a BA in Sculpture. Her work sits between sculpture, costume and the body, using these forms to explore emotion, identity and the human condition. She often works collaboratively with dancers and performers, creating sculptural pieces that are moved with, worn or interacted with.

In addition to her performance-based practice, Carolina creates participatory workshops inspired by her collaborative projects, inviting the audience into a more intimate and embodied dialogue.

VIVIAN GABEL | Choreographer

Vivian is a Peruvian dancer and choreographer whose journey began with a decade of classical ballet training before transitioning into Hip Hop and Dancehall in 2013. A former member of Spirit Hop and co-founder of Vanilla Dancehall Crew, winners of the Dancehall Master World in Paris 2018.

She choreographed the award-winning music video *El año del Conejo Chino by Kanaku y el Tigre* (Best Peruvian Video, 2020). Her commercial work includes campaigns and flash mobs for Universal Studios Peru and other major brands, bringing performance to the public in bold and unexpected ways. Vivian is currently choreographing Peru's first national LGBTIQ+ reggaetón cast for *The Ministry of Beauty*, and developing *80's Sinfónico*, a large-scale musical at the Gran Teatro Nacional del Perú.

Vivian's academic background in Philosophy and Education informs both her creative vision and her compassionate, empowering teaching and directing style.

TOM CAGNONI | Musical Supervisor & Orchestrator

Tom is a Musical Director, Composer, Orchestrator, Producer and Performer. He originally trained in jazz guitar before studying Maths & Music at The University of Leeds.

His recent credits as Musical Director include: *Billie The Kid* at the Vaudeville Theatre and Musical Supervisor/Composer and *Miss Brexit* at Omnibus Clapham.

Tom has also worked extensively with OVO Theatre over the past 8 years as a Musical Director and Composer with his credits including *A Midsummer Night's Dream*, *Romeo & Juliet*, *Little Women*, *The Railway Children*, *A Christmas Carol*, *The Importance of Being Earnest*, *Les Liaisons Dangereuses*, *The Winter's Tale*, and *Peter Pan* among others.

ALEJANDRO CLAVIER | Dramaturg

Alejandro is a Lima-based Venezuelan-Peruvian interdisciplinary artist working across theatre, film, and curation. Since 2013, he has directed Sala de Parto (Delivery Room), Teatro La Plaza's platform for emerging performing artists, focused on developing bold, contemporary Peruvian work. The current edition, co-directed with Claudia Tangoa, supports women, nonbinary, and gender-nonconforming artists through a long-term process involving mentorship, workshops, and funding. Sala de Parto also includes an annual festival featuring these new works alongside local and international productions.

His work has been presented in festivals across Peru, Argentina, Chile, Brazil, Panama, and Northern Ireland. In 2019, he joined a delegation of young Latin American theatre directors at the Festival d'Avignon. Notable projects include *Simón, el topo*, a puppet play on family dialogue and queerness; *Allin Willakuykuna*, a transmedia piece on resilience commissioned by the Red Cross; and *San Bartolo*, shortlisted for Theatertreffen's Stückemarkt.

CHARACTERS

MIGUEL & GABRIEL – Narrators of the story. Half archangels, half go-go girls

JESÚS – A super Catholic altar boy on his way to his first communion, played by the actor that plays **MIGUEL**

All others played by the actor that plays **GABRIEL**:

MOTHER MARÍA – Tender and a bit ditsy. Jesús' mom.

LIEUTENANT JOSÉ – Macho and tough-loving. Jesús' dad.

FATHER ANGELO – Creepy school priest. Passionate about sex-ed.

COUSIN – Athletic and American. His Spanish is shit.

JEEZUS – The son of God. He's got daddy issues.

SETTING

Lima, Perú,
and Jesús' auntie's house in Orlando, Florida ("BAPTISM").

TIME

The '90s.

NOTE ON MUSIC

(♫♫♫) means background music
(♫ JEEZUS! ♫) is a musical sound effect

SUNG LYRICS
ARE IN ALL CAPS

AUTHOR'S NOTE

by Sergio Antonio Maggiolo

JEEZUS! was born from an outrageous question: How do I turn the trauma of growing up queer in conservative Catholic Latin America... into a musical comedy?

This show is not here to mock religion. It's here to wrestle with it. With all its contradictions, ecstasies, hypocrisies, and power. I grew up in a part of South America where religion was more than dogma. It was a pillar of identity. A language for love, for family, for community. But like many queer people, I learned early that that love came with conditions. That faith could be a door – or a wall.

JEEZUS! takes place in a surreal, camp, and filthy theatrical universe. Two divine narrators, MIGUEL and GABRIEL (half archangels, half go-go dancers), guide us through the story of Jesús, a super Catholic Peruvian altar boy on his way to his first communion, and his unexpected queer awakening, triggered by none other than a very sexy Jeezus Christ.

You'll notice the spelling: Jesús is the boy (pronounced heh-SOOS), and Jeezus is the son of God. The distinction matters. Jesús is always portrayed as a child, even though he's played by an adult actor. The sexual elements of the show come from adult reflection on childhood shame and desire, not from the child himself. It's part of the play's central tension: how can someone so young, so devout, so desperate to be "good," navigate desire when the only model of divinity is a tortured, hypermasculine man nailed to a cross?

This show is absurd, joyful, and brutal. It's also a love letter — to queerness, to myth, to the kids who thought they were going to hell. I wrote it with my real-life partner, Guido, and we perform it together as a two-person act of divine mischief and radical tenderness. And at its heart, it's not really about God. It's about the stories we inherit, the bodies we live in, and the miracles we make for ourselves.

We're so glad you're here. Whether you came for the blasphemy, the music, or the foot fetish jokes, bienvenidx. You are a miracle. I'm here for you.

— Sergio

THANK YOU FROM THE TEAM

To the institutions and venues that supported the project from the beginning:

To Brian Logan who first believed in the idea and everyone at CPT who made us feel welcome when we were developing our first work in progress.

To Southwark Council, the Southwark I Create program and Michelle Walker that were the first funders of *JEEZUS!*

To Bryony Kimmings and the group of artists that experienced the earliest development workshop.

To Theatre Peckham and the Canada Water Library for supporting us with rehearsal space and early dramaturgical support.

To Summerhall, their Summerhall Surgeries program and Tom Foster for planting the seed of us taking *JEEZUS!* to Edinburgh Fringe

To the Arts Council England for helping us fund the step-up into a musical and Alex Etchart for helping us find the right words to secure that support.

To The Pleasance and Nic Connaughton for believing in the play and allowing us to have a home in London.

To Brixton House, eStage and the team of Housemates festival for letting us flourish and learn in their venue.

To the people that have offered their work and help throughout the years:

Hector Manchego, Nico Lejtrejer, Chander van Daatselaar, Shelton Lindsay, Marco Vigilante, Miguel Torres Umba, Donnacadh O'Briain, Florian Lim, Nevi Pepa Duarte, Giancarlo Ferrini, Eduardo Arcelus, Francisco Diaz, Mariana Aristizábal, Malena Arcucci, Ephemeral Ensemble, Chusi Amorós and Rio.

To Mark Pether, Evelyn Connor, Tom Killeen, Jana Nightingale, Zoë Billingham, Jan Ryan, Cecilia Darker, Adriana Ducassi and Dominic Rampston.

To Frida Hurtado, Julio Marcone, José Miguel Maggiolo, Mercedes Oropeza, Cristóbal, Emilio y el que está en camino. Vanessa Vizcarra, Bruno Espejo, Justina, Lxs Valientes, Las Moscas, Los Locuaz, Los lonchecitos de los miércoles and Charles Tuthill.

To Mel García, Pilar Lueches, Daniel García and Agustín Maggi.

And to my parents Ana Maria Bogino and Eugenio Maggiolo who only ever showed me love.

GENESIS

*(Darkness. Thunder and Wind. A chorus of susurrations whispering 'Jeezus' again and again. We hear the musical motif of **"The Lord Of The Miracles".**)*

GABRIEL.

In a land that no one cares about

at least not in the west

MIGUEL.

A holy territory

of political unrest

GABRIEL.

A Miracle manifested

and made this place *divine*

MIGUEL.

The village: Bethlehem

in present day, ...Lima, Perú

GABRIEL. Where else were you thinking, boo?

(Thunder strikes.)

MIGUEL.

A woman called María –

GABRIEL.

That's Mary to you.

MIGUEL.

Married Corporal José,

GABRIEL.

That's Joseph...

MIGUEL.

They get it.

GABRIEL.

They do.

(♫♫♫)

They longed to have a blessed child

And just could not conceive

MIGUEL.

But there are powers beyond medicine

And María Believed in

MARÍA.

THE LORD OF THE MIRACLES...

MIGUEL.

The local Jeezus Fucking Christ

GABRIEL.

An ancient mural painting

Of a god that's not quite white

MIGUEL.

Armed with diamonds and a purple cloak

María went to the church

Knelt before the painting of Jeezus

Took a breath and said:

MARÍA.

LORD OF THE MIRACLES

IF YOU GIVE A MIRACLE

I'LL LIVE FOR YOU
YOU MAY HAVE ALL THESE RICHES
I'LL NEVER TAKE OFF THIS PURPLE SUIT

MIGUEL & GABRIEL.

THE LORD CONSIDERS HER BARGAIN
DIAMONDS AND WORSHIP IN EXCHANGE FOR A LIFE
AND LET'S FACE IT...
DIAMONDS MAKE HIS BIG DICK HARD

MIGUEL.

HIS HOLY IMMATERIAL SPIRIT SHOOTS OUT FROM THE
    PAINTING ON THE WALL
AND PENETRATES MARÍA'S UTERUS WITH DIVINE
    FERTILIZER.

MIGUEL & GABRIEL.

JEEZUS!

MIGUEL.

HER BODY IS OVERWHELMED BY RAPTURE
AS THE IMMACULATE CONCEPTION BEGINS.

MIGUEL & GABRIEL.

JEEZUS!

MIGUEL.

THE DIAMONDS ARE SUBLIMATED INTO PURE AIR
AND A NEW SOUL GIGGLES IN HEAVEN.

MIGUEL & GABRIEL.

JEEZUS!

MARÍA.

I'LL NAME THIS BOY...

Jesús.

MIGUEL & GABRIEL.

NOT JEEZUS BUT JESÚS
SOON TO BE PERU'S MESSIAH
IN A PATH WITH NO CLUES, TO CHOOSE
BETWEEN SIN AND ETERNAL FIRE

MIGUEL & GABRIEL.

    A SUPER CATHOLIC ALTAR BOY
    READY FOR THE BODY OF THE CHRIST
    DETERMINED TO LET GO OF THE THINGS
    JEEZUS SACRIFICED

JESÚS.

    I WANNA BE THE CHOSEN
    TO FULFILL MY DADDY'S PLAN
    I'LL MAKE MY FIRST COMMUNION
    AND EXTEND GOD'S LOVE TO EVERY MAN

MIGUEL & GABRIEL.

    THE STORY OF JESÚS
    SOON TO BE PERU'S MESSIAH
    IN A PATH WITH NO CLUES, TO CHOOSE
    BETWEEN SIN AND ETERNAL FIRE

    IN A PATH WITH NO CLUES, TO CHOOSE
    BETWEEN SIN AND ETERNAL FIRE

BAPTISM

MIGUEL. Jesús is now one month away from his first communion.

GABRIEL. And as the big day approaches, María and José take him on a trip to the holiest land in the whole world:

MIGUEL. Orlando, Florida!

GABRIEL. They're going for their once-in-a-lifetime pilgrimage to the birthplace of Prophet Mickey Mouse and to celebrate Easter with María's sister and her family who immigrated there years ago.

MIGUEL. The grown-ups are very excited to catch up downstairs. So they bring some milk and cookies to Jesús and his newly-acquainted cousin and leave them to *'entertain themselves'*.

COUSIN. Daddy says Perú is very poor.

JESÚS. Qué?

COUSIN. *Pa-pah* dees-ey que Puh-roo ez moo-cho, *poor.*

JESÚS. Eh... I speak English.

COUSIN. Thank God 'cause my Spanish is shit!

JESÚS. Noh, noh. Is nice! – Your hair is so long. And you have an earring?!

COUSIN. You're cute. I'll be back.

   (He exits.)

JESÚS. God Bless America. Wow, this room is full of first-world stuff. A Nintendo 64. M&M's.* A crucifix with an electronic Jeezus that resurrects when you press the button!

---

* A licence to produce *JEEZUS!* does not include a licence to publicly display any branded logos or trademarked images. Licensees must acquire rights for any logos and/or images or create their own.

(♫ JEEZUS! ♫)

JESÚS. I love him! Trophies my cousin has won in swimming competitions and pictures of other white boys in speedos, and a collection of VHS tapes: *Mulan... Silence of the Lambs... Charmed* Season Three?!* ...And there's this one tape. With a blank case. Nothing written on it. Strange. So I put it on the giant TV and I sit on the bed.

(♫♫♫)

GABRIEL. The film opens with a knock at the door and a woman opening it: Oh! It's the plumber.

JESÚS. He's got long shiny hair like my cousin.

GABRIEL. She unbuttons her blouse as the pipeman licks her nipples.

JESÚS. His tongue is big. And his face is strong and pretty.

GABRIEL. A cinematic fade into their fully naked bodies very close to each other. His huge hands holding her from behind, his sweaty skin that seems to glisten under the artificial light.

JESÚS. I'm in awe of his giant...feet, and his lower half pushing against hers.

GABRIEL & JESÚS. Boom, Boom, Boom

JESÚS. I wish I could...

I hear someone coming. But before I have time to reset everything, my cousin enters the room! Oh Jeezus! He's come back from the shower. Wrapped in a towel.

My fourteen-year-old, professional-swimmer, American cousin wrapped in a towel enters the room!

---

* A licence to produce *JEEZUS!* does not include a licence to publicly display any branded logos or trademarked images. Licensees must acquire rights for any logos and/or images or create their own.

HE LOOKS AT THE TV, SURPRISED – BEMUSED,
A BIT LAUGHTER WITH URGENCY INFUSED,
HE FUMBLES DRIPPING I WANT TO RUN AWAY,
BUT I STAY THERE, WATCHING HIS BULGE SWAY

HE SPEAKS TO ME – BUT I DON'T UNDERSTAND,
MY LITTLE MIND FIXED ON HIS GIANT WET HANDS,
HIS TWO MASSIVE FEET – NO SOCK
AND THE DARK PATCH GROWING ABOVE HIS...BELLY
BUTTON
THEN MY PUPILS ENLARGE LIKE THOSE OF AN OWL
HE COMES NEAR TO ME AND NONCHALANTLY DROPS HIS
TOWEL
AND IN THAT MOMENT I'VE BEEN SET FREE
LIKE EVE, I'VE EATEN...
I'VE EATEN THE FRUIT FROM THE TREE

LIKE EVE, LIKE EVE, LIKE EVE, LIKE EVE,
I'VE EATEN THE FRUIT FROM THE TREE
LIKE EVE, LIKE EVE, LIKE EVE, LIKE EVE,
I'VE EATEN THE FRUIT!

LIKE AN ANIMAL I MOVE 'ROUND CARELESS
GETTING CLOSER HIS FEET: TEMPTING, BIG AND
HAIRLESS
I INSTINCTIVELY LAY ON THEM MY FACE FLAT,
I SMELL AND KISS 'EM – ANYTHING WRONG WITH THAT?!

PRESSING MY FACE TO HIS SOLES STILL WET-ISH
I HOLD TIGHT AS I DEVELOP MY FIRST FETISH
YOU PULL BACK... AWKWARD SILENCE FILLS THE AIR

COUSIN.

THE MOVIE HUMMING IN THE BACKGROUND LIKE A
PRAYER
WE'RE HALFWAY THERE
YOU AND ME CUZ, LIVING ON A PRAYER

JESÚS. I feel like I'm doing something cheeky. But then
I see him. He's hung. On the wall... Nailed to the
electronic cross. Jeezus holds my gaze His long shiny

hair, his beautiful naked body, his eyes that seem to say
"Go on Jesús"... And then –

    *(♫ **JEEZUS!** ♫)*

– he winks at me!

COUSIN.

  NOW YOU'VE RELAXED

JESÚS.

  AND UNBURDENED ME OF PRESSURE

COUSIN & JESÚS.

  AND I SUCCUMB AND EXPERIENCE THIS DIVINE
    TREASURE
  OF THE LORD'S WORD, AM I BEING A TRANSGRESSOR?
  BUT I AM FULL NOW! I'VE GIVEN MYSELF UP TO
    PLEASURE.

  LIKE EVE, LIKE EVE, LIKE EVE, LIKE EVE,
  I'VE EATEN THE FRUIT FROM THE TREE
  MY FEET, MY FEET, MY FEET, MY FEET
  I'VE GIVEN MYSELF UP TO PLEASURE.
  LIKE EVE, LIKE EVE, LIKE EVE, LIKE EVE,
  I JUST WANNA EAT THAT FRUIT
  MY FEET, MY FEET, MY FEET, MY FEET
  I'VE GIVEN MYSELF UP TO PLEASURE.

    *(They take a big gulp of milk and wipe it off
    their faces.)*

THE COMMANDMENTS

MIGUEL. Back-to-mucho-poor Peru

GABRIEL & MIGUEL. The Holy Trinity Academy...Church School...For Boys

GABRIEL. Only one week until all the boys in year six take their first communion

MIGUEL. Jesús is nervous because today they'll announce who's been chosen to be the altar boy for the first communion ceremony, and he really, *really* wants it. We find him in Biology class with Father Angelo: Part priest, part science teacher, part auntie.

FATHER ANGELO. Ready Jesús?

JESÚS. Yes, Father!

FATHER ANGELO & JESÚS.
>LET'S BE...THANKFUL TO THE LORD.
>LET'S BE THANKFUL!
>LET'S BE THANKFUL TO THE LORD
>LET'S BE THANKFUL TO THE LORD.
>LET'S BE THANKFUL!
>LET'S BE –

FATHER ANGELO. Did you masturbate last night??! Confess!!

JESÚS. Remember God can read our thoughts! Cast our filthy sins away, almighy Jeezus! Clean the soul of us sinners!

FATHER ANGELO. Amen, Jesús! Follow Father's orders! Fight *the devil* who is always trying to tempt you, boys. You are the new soldiers of God! Marching towards your first communion!

JESÚS. Amen!

FATHER ANGELO & JESÚS.

>THREE LITTLE BIRDS, SING EVERY MORNING
>BEAUTIFUL PRAISES FOR JEEZUS DIED FOR YOU...

JESÚS.

>DIED FOR YOU!

FATHER ANGELO & JESÚS.

>BROTHERS AND SIBLINGS... WHY AREN'T YOU SINGING?
>BEAUTIFUL PRAISES FOR JEEZUS DIED FOR YOU...

JESÚS.

>DIED FOR YOU!

FATHER ANGELO. Don't think about my genitals! I see you thinking about my genitals!

JESÚS. Not me! Who?! Aha! Rosita, of course.

FATHER ANGELO. The devil *craves* for you to partake in Mortal Sin, boys! Lust... Murder... Reggaeton.

JESÚS. We shall clean properly before you come inside of us, Jeezus! "For thou shalt confess thy sins to the older man in the dark booth in great graphic detail and thou shalt be fixed!" Leviticus 68–69.

FATHER ANGELO & JESÚS.

>BROTHERS AND SIBLINGS, WHY AREN'T YOU SINGING?
>BEAUTIFUL PRAISES FOR JEEZUS DIED FOR YOU...

JESÚS.

>DIED FOR YOU!
>LET'S BE –

FATHER ANGELO. Hands up, who's put something up their butthole? Hmmm... That's the most Mortal Sin of them all, boys... Feel shame and repent before it's too late! If you take your first communion with a Mortal Sin God will kill your soul and send you to burn in hell.

(Bell tolls.)

Saved by the bell. Jesús, you've proven to be a very precocious little boy. You are the chosen altar boy for the first communion!

JESÚS. AHHHHH...

FATHER ANGELO. Jeezus is clearly pleased with you! Now it is written! You shall eat his flesh and become a brand new vessel!

JESÚS. "And Jeezus will thrust in my mortar his mighty pestle".

FATHER ANGELO. Yes. Yes he will. Now, everyone don't forget to watch the film *The Life of Jeezus: The Movie.* The whole six hours of it! And DO NOT HAVE FUN. Remember: Jeezus died for you, so...

FATHER ANGELO & JESÚS.

LET'S BE THANKFUL TO THE LORD!

THE PROMISED LAND

MIGUEL. Jesús gets picked up from The Holy Trinity Academy Church School...for Boys! By his father, Sergeant José.

GABRIEL.. Hem-hem

MIGUEL. Sorry! ...Lieutenant José! He's just been promoted!

GABRIEL. And by president Fujimori himself! For being an example of obedience and sacrifice in the fight against the evil forces of terrorism.

MIGUEL. Lieutenant José *loves* President Fujimori

GABRIEL. And he's been making a huge deal about wanting his son to be chosen as the altar boy.

MIGUEL. So Jesús is excited, a bit relieved and just about to share the news when the car screeches to a halt, blocked by a street protest.

JOSÉ. Agh! Go protest somewhere else! TERRORISTAS!

JESÚS. What's that red flag with the hammer, Dad?

JOSÉ. It's the symbol of the devil, Jesús. We have to be careful, any of these agitators can be a terrorist. These cowards are afraid 'cause they know the Americans are coming to help us win this war.

JESÚS. We're on the side of God *and America*?! We're definitely gonna win!

JOSÉ. Amen.

JESÚS. Dad? I was chosen to be the altar boy!

JOSÉ. At your first communion?! Fuck yeah! I mean... Well done, Jesús! That makes me very proud of you.

JESÚS. I get to lead the final prayer...and sing in the choir...

JOSÉ. And on the day of your Abuela's birthday, what a miracle!

JESÚS. Father Angelo told me Jeezus is very pleased with me!

JOSÉ. Of course he is, son. His love is your reward for following His word.

JESÚS. He promoted me just like the President did with you!

JOSÉ. You're learning what it means to be a man, Jesús: We obey the commands to protect what we love. You know if it weren't for Fujimori this country would still be the same mess it was when I was your age... Did I ever tell you about – *blablablablabla*

  (♫ ♫ ♫)

MIGUEL. And this is when Lieutenant José rants about the Old Peruvian Agrarian Revolution and the Current Internal Armed Conflict:

GABRIEL. It's all a bit dry.

MIGUEL. Basically: Peru's got some heavy Papi Issues.

GABRIEL. Let us juice up the historical context

MIGUEL. 1960s... Let's Go!

MIGUEL & GABRIEL.

  MY INNER POPULATION
  FED UP OF SUBJUGATION
  DEMANDS REDISTRIBUTION
  INSIDE SUGAR PLANTATIONS

  FIX THE SOUL OF MY NATION
  PAY BILLIONS IN REPARATIONS
  THE SOLUTION: REVOLUTION
  PRINT MY RIGHTS IN YOUR CONSTITUTION

MIGUEL & GABRIEL.

> WHO'S YOUR FUCKING PAPI? – COLONIALISM
> WHO YOU FUCKING, PAPI? – FEUDALISM
> WANNA FUCK ME, PAPI? – YES! COMMUNISM!
> WHAT?! DID WE SAY COMMUNISM?
>
> PAPI PAPI PAPI U.S.A.
> PAPI PAPI WANNA PLAY?
> PAPI PAPI PAPI COUP D'ETAT
> GIMME GIMME GIMME GIMME SOME OF THAT
>
> PAPI PAPI PAPI FUJIMORI
> MY BODY IS YOUR TERRITORY
> PAPI PAPI PAPI FATHERLAND
> GIMME GIMME GIMME YOUR COMMAND
>
> 1990s – LET'S GO!
>
> INEQUALITY 'COMES BRUTALITY
> KILL THE TERRORISTS AND THEIR FAMILIES
> PRIVATIZE MY MINES AND WATERS
> SNORT MY COCAINE RAPE MY DAUGHTERS
>
> MAKE YOUR MEDIA INFLUENCING
> PERPETRATE SOME ETHNIC CLEANSING
> RIG ELECTIONS, TAKE YOUR PICK
> WE WILL SUCK YOUR MASSIVE DICK–
> –TATORSHIP

GABRIEL.

> Take me to the bridge –

MIGUEL.

> Oh no. We can't.

GABRIEL.

> Why not?

MIGUEL.

> The Terrorist blew it up!

MIGUEL & GABRIEL.

      PAPI PAPI PAPI U.S.A.

      PAPI I'LL OBEY, OBEY, OBEY

      PAPI PAPI PAPI COUP D'ETAT

      GIMME GIMME GIMME GIMME SOME OF THAT

      PAPI PAPI PAPI FUJIMORI

      MY BODY IS YOUR TERRITORY

      PAPI PAPI PAPI FATHERLAND

      GIMME GIMME GIMME YOUR CUM–

      GIMME GIMME GIMME YOUR CUM–

      GIMME GIMME GIMME YOUR COMMAND

THE LAST SUPPER

GABRIEL. Abuela's House in the Outskirts of Lima. Bethlehem Military Village where Jesús is growing up.

MIGUEL. A sacred home passed down through generations. Every room guarded by an image of The Lord of the Miracles:

MIGUEL & GABRIEL. The local Jeezus Fucking Christ

MIGUEL. The whole family gathers to celebrate Abuela's birthday. She's in the middle of the table as a centerpiece in an urn. She's been dead for years.

GABRIEL. At the table there's Jesús and twelve others. For some reason they all sat on the same side...

MIGUEL. Mother María. She's wearing the same purple cloak she wears every day of her life. It's so camp!

GABRIEL. They're eating Abuela's favorite dish –

MIGUEL. Allegedly!

GABRIEL. Chicken with prunes and pickled turnips

MIGUEL. It's disgusting. The only one who seems to be enjoying it is Sergeant José... Sorry! Lieutenant José.

GABRIEL. He's talking about terrorist groups committing massacres in rural Peru, and the soldiers who are sacrificing their lives in the fight against them.

MIGUEL. Last night, in a remote city in the Amazon, a mob entered a queer bar, murdered eight gay teenagers and displayed their corpses in the main square.

GABRIEL. It is the first time Jesús hears his family talking about homosexuality.

MIGUEL. Such a lovely conversation to have over dinner.

MIGUEL & GABRIEL.
> SUPPER CHAT!
> BLESS OUR FOOD
> DELIVER US FROM THOSE WHO

JESÚS.
> LIKE EVE, LIKE EVE, LIKE EVE...

JOSÉ. ...They had it coming! It was a nasty dive bar full of faggots.

JESÚS. Faggots? ...What's a faggot?

MARÍA. Nothing Jesúsito, just keep eating. Language!

JOSÉ. I mean they brought it on themselves. Living like that in Mortal sin.

JOSÉ & JESÚS.
> SIN, SIN, SIN, SIN

JESÚS. So, a faggot is...a Mortal Sinner?

JOSÉ. Oh Yes. Yes they are.

JESÚS. So say I stole Rosita's eraser. Not that I have of course! But that wouldn't make me a faggot, right?

JOSÉ. Don't say that, son! No! A faggot is a...a queer. A fruit. A sissy...

JOSÉ & JESÚS.
> SIS-SY – SIS-SY

MARÍA. José!

JESÚS. A sissy –? What do you mean, Dad?

MARÍA. Let me take this one. A... A

JESÚS. Faggot...

MARÍA. Yes...is a man who wants to be a woman. There.

JESÚS. So like...wearing dresses?

JOSÉ. More like having filthy, homo, sexual deviations –

JOSÉ & JESÚS.

> SEX – UP – THE – BUM

MARÍA. José!

JOSÉ. What? Lots of them in the army! I'd rather my son was a terrorist than a faggot. You need to learn what to stay away from.

JESÚS. Yes, Dad.

JOSÉ. "The very touch or desire from one man to another shall be deemed as Mortal Sin punished by the devil's anal impalement –"

JESÚS. Anal imp–

MARÍA. José!

JESÚS. QUÉ?!

MARÍA. No! Really, José? ...Anal impalement? ...Jesús, why don't you tell your aunties about your First Communion on Sunday?

JESÚS. Ehhh...yeah, we're all wearing white dresses.

MARÍA. Ave María Purísima!

JOSÉ. And you have been chosen to be the altar boy! He'll be leading the closing prayer at the ceremony.

JESÚS. – I feel something's wrong.

JOSÉ. I want to give you this, a gift from your Abuela on her birthday

JESÚS. Thanks, Dad, but –

JOSÉ. Her "Lord of the Miracles" medallion. A symbol of our family. Put it on!

JESÚS. Oh no, I really shouldn't –

JOSÉ. Why don't you lead a prayer before we toast to her?

JESÚS. No Dad, I think I'm –

JOSÉ. Do what you're told. She'd love you praying for –

JESÚS. Dad, please I don't want to –

JOSÉ. Don't be a sissy, Jesús, come on! –

JESÚS. I don't want to make my First Communion!

> *(Pause.)*

MARÍA. Hahaha! You little devil! We almost fell for that, didn't we? Hilarious! Those wine glasses could use a refill, no? Top-up your aunties, Jesús, go on.

JESÚS. Lieutenant José stares at me. Am I a F– Mortal Sinner? Did I only imagine Jeezus winking at me? What is Anal Impalement? Whatever it is I need to clean myself before Sunday or I'll burn in hell! My father doesn't speak, but I obey him 'cause I know exactly what he's thinking.

JOSÉ.

OH JESÚS

JESÚS.

"In the name of the Father, and of the Son, and the Holy Spirit..."

JOSÉ.

MY FIRST BORN

JESÚS.

"Thy Kingdom come, Thy will be done"

JOSÉ.

YOU NEED TO CLEANSE YOURSELF FROM

JESÚS.

"But deliver us from evil –"

> *(The medallion begins to bleed red wine. It pours from Jesús' body: painful, but purging. During the song, he serves it to the audience. A strange, ritualistic communion)*

JOSÉ.

    SIN, SIN, SIN, SIN
    YOUR MORTAL SIN
    YOUR SICKLY, FOUL DISORDER

    ABUELA'S WISH WAS
    THAT YOU AND ME
    BECOME GOD'S HOLY SOLDIERS

    IT'S WHO YOU ARE
    OUR COVENANT
    TO BEAR UPON YOUR SHOULDERS

    ACCEPT THE PAIN
    ENDURE THE SHAME
    THESE ARE YOUR FATHER'S ORDERS:

    YOU'LL EAT HIS FLESH
    YOU'LL DRINK HIS BLOOD
    YOU'LL MAKE YOUR FIRST COMMUNION

    BECOME A MAN
    AND SACRIFICE
    FULFILL GOD AND MAN'S UNION

    LEAD THE DAMN PRAYER
    OR YOU'LL RUIN
    THIS FAMILY REUNION

    OBEY THE RULES
    DO AS YOU'RE TOLD
    AND PROMISE US THAT YOU WON'T BE A FILTHY FAAAAG

A toast! To Jesús becoming a man. Amen.

JESÚS. Amen.

THE GOSPEL ACCORDING TO MARÍA

MIGUEL & GABRIEL. Ah-Men!

MIGUEL. Straight Men!

GABRIEL. Straight Military Men!

MIGUEL. Straight Homophobic Military Men!

GABRIEL. They are so obsessed with gay people, just like the priests.

MIGUEL. I think it's because they didn't get enough of it in the barracks, you know?

"Oh! Lieutenant Sergeant, I think you dropped your soap."

GABRIEL. *"Oh! Private Ryan! What are you gonna do about it?"*

MIGUEL. *"Maybe I'll pick it up...or maybe I'll lick your anus."*

GABRIEL & GABRIEL. *"Ahh! AHHH!"*

(Thunder.)

MIGUEL. But we digress...

GABRIEL. Dinner is done. And the aunties leave early because of the nightly curfew.

MIGUEL. María wants a word with José in the kitchen so Jesusito goes back upstairs feeling upset.

GABRIEL. Hard to say if it was the pickled turnips or the fear of God killing his soul.

MIGUEL. To cheer up he likes to sneak into María's closet to try on some expensive jewelry.

GABRIEL. He usually wears his favourite pair of earrings that used to belong to Abuela. Two big golden crosses, each missing a teardrop-shaped diamond in the centre.

MIGUEL. But tonight, he's unsure of what to do with them. He's just quietly contemplating them when suddenly –

MARÍA. Jesús, you're here –!

JESÚS. Mom!

MARÍA. I saw you were a bit nervous at dinner. Are you alright?

JESÚS. I'm fine.

MARÍA. I hate that chicken too...

> *(Beat.)*

Are they calling you that ugly name at school again?

JESÚS. No, Mom. Everything's fine.

MARÍA. You can tell me anything Jesús...

JESÚS. It's... It's about my First Communion. I don't want to disappoint anyone.

MARÍA. My love, I know your father can be a bit harsh at times but he loves you very much.

JESÚS. I know, Mom.

MARÍA. We'll all be there to support you.

JESÚS. I know.

MARÍA. So, what is it then?

JESÚS. It's just that... I think I'm – I think I'm not good enough.

MARÍA. What do you mean? You're amazing! The way you sing that "Baby one more time" song –

JESÚS. I don't mean being good at singing, Mom. I mean... Father Angelo told us about Mortal Sins that can kill our souls.

MARÍA. Well...they call them *deadly* for a reason. But you don't have to worry about that. You can always talk to Jeezus, he loves you very much.

JESÚS. But what if Jeezus is also disappointed in me? And doesnt love me anymore?

  (Beat.)

MARÍA. Did I ever tell you what happened to the diamonds in these earrings?

JESÚS. Yes Mom! Many times...

MARÍA. Well I don't care, you listen again because obviously you weren't paying attention! Me and your father wanted to have you so badly, Jesús, but every doctor told us we would never be able to get pregnant. Until your Abuela convinced me to go see the painting of –

MARÍA & JESÚS. – *The Lord of the Miracles*...

MARÍA. And I promised him: "If you give me a son within a year, I will give you the most valuable thing I own and I will wear your purple cloak for the rest of my life." And before the year was out, you were born.

 YOU ARE A MIRACLE...
 YOU ARE MY MIRACLE, I'M HERE FOR YOU

Jeezus gave you life, Jesús. He loves you exactly for who you are.

JESÚS. But what if I'm not who he expects me to be? Will he stop giving me his love?

MARÍA. When somebody loves you, they don't give you anything. When somebody loves you, a new part of them is born inside of you. And there it lives, and grows, and it stays a part of you forever. It's like my love for you, Jesús. No one can ever take that away.

(Beat.)

JESÚS. Tomorrow after school, can you take me to see *The Lord of the Miracles*? I want to ask him something.

REVELATIONS

JESÚS.
IN MY COUNTRY THERE'S A PAINTING
MADE WITH BRUSHSTROKES OF RESISTANCE
AND THROUGH CENTURIES OF RESILIENCE
MIRACLES FABRICATING

SPAIN INVADED, KILLED AND RAVAGED
EMPIRE WHERE THE SUN DON'T SET
THEY TOOK ALL THEY COULD GET,
GAVE US GOD, EL ESPAÑOL AND THEIR SLAVE TRADE.
SO SAVAGE.

WHITE LORDS KEPT CONTROL
FARMING COTTON, GOLD AND BIRD SHITS
AND THOSE BROUGHT HERE ON THEIR SHIPS
PAINTED A BROWN JEEZUS ON A WALL

LORD OF THE MIRACLES
LORD OF THE MIRACLES
THEY'RE HERE FOR YOU
CAN'T YOU SEE THEM WAITING
KNEEL BEFORE YOUR PAINTING
FOR YOUR TRUTH

GABRIEL. The procession of The Lord of The Miracles, the biggest Catholic demonstration in the Americas. Amidst the mass of people Jesús walks into the same church that María entered years ago. Kneels before the painting and closes his eyes praying for help...

IT'S A PAINTING OF BROWN JEEZUS
TALK ABOUT AVANT-GARDE REPRESENTATION
'CAUSE WHEN STOLEN FROM OUR NATION
IT'S OUR FAITH IN HIM THAT FREES US

FOR CENTURIES THIS WALL STOOD
THROUGH EARTHQUAKES, DEMOLITION ATTEMPTS
REMINDING US THAT WHEN THE DEVIL TEMPTS
THE FORCE OF CHRIST IS A SHIELD OF GOOD

JESÚS.

    LORD OF THE MIRACLES
    LORD OF THE MIRACLES
    I'M HERE FOR YOU

    CAN'T YOU SEE ME WAITING
    KNEEL BEFORE YOUR PAINTING
    FOR YOUR TRUTH

GABRIEL. Jesús stares at *The Lord of the Miracles*, and he sees them...two identical teardrop-shaped diamonds encrusted in his oil-painted cheeks. Suddenly, a beam of light shoots out from the painting on the wall and penetrates Jesús deep inside his soul...

    (♫ JEEZUS! ♫)

...His body is overwhelmed by rapture as the revelation begins...

JESÚS.

    LORD OF THE MIRACLES I NEED AN EMPIRICAL ANSWER
        FROM YOU
    SHOULD I BE REPENTING?
    OR SHOULD I FOLLOW WHAT'S TEMPTING BUT IS TRUE?

JEEZUS. "It's inside you, Jesús."

JESÚS. What the fuck

CONFIRMATION

MIGUEL.
GUESS WHO'S BACK IN THE HOUSE!
JESÚS BACK IN THE HOUSE!
JESÚS BACK IN ABUELA'S HOUSE!

Jesús is back in Abuela's House.

GABRIEL. The first communion is tomorrow! María and José have made sure Jesús is super ready to fulfill his duties as altar boy! Sing in the choir, light the candles, wear the silky white dress. And the family's favorite! Passing the collection basket: five, six, seven, eight!

JESÚS.
MONEY, MONEY, MONEY!
GIVE ME MONEY!
WE HAVE A QR CODE!

I only have twenty-four hours to get rid of my Mortal Sin! And I haven't even watched *The Life of Jeezus: The Movie* – the whole six hours of it! Surely there's something there that can help me follow his word! So I grab the VHS tape from the shelf, I put it on the giant TV and sit on the bed.

(♪♪♪)

GABRIEL. The Film opens with who should be a Middle Eastern man, but he's white and blond and his face is strong and pretty.

JESÚS. He's walking to several groups of hunky men and promising them eternal love if they leave everything they have behind and follow him. And they do!

GABRIEL. They go on adventures and have deep talks in caves, and wash each other's feet and it's wonderful.

JESÚS. But the real sexy bit is when one of the hunks kisses hot blond Jeezus on the mouth and a homophobic

Roman Guard comes and arrests him and sentences him to flogging. So they strip him down, and he is a hottie.

GABRIEL. They tie his wrists to a pole, and start flogging his robust back. His carpenter muscles tighten but his face is unyielding, he's taking it like a boss.

JESÚS. Is this normal? That it turns me on?

GABRIEL. As if that wasn't sexy enough. He is made to parade the streets wearing only a loincloth, while people spit in his face so his white skin is covered by a mix of sweat and spit.

JESÚS. Which also turns me on a little bit.

GABRIEL. Finally he's humiliated, manhandled and nailed to a cross.

GABRIEL & JESÚS. Boom, Boom, Boom

JESÚS. Every hammer blow unleashes a deep erotic moan, which in turn unleashes my sadomasochistic pubertal imagination. His undeniable six-pack manifesting as he asphyxiates to death. Is this fucked up?

JEEZUS. *"Jesús. Let's goooo."*

GABRIEL.
    LIKE EVE, LIKE EVE, LIKE EVE,

JESÚS. I look at the crucifix in my room.

GABRIEL.
    LIKE EVE, LIKE EVE, LIKE EVE

JESÚS. And I take it off the wall
    OH JEEZUS
    I WANT YOU TO SPLIT ME OPEN
    LIKE AN APPLE
    AND BURY YOUR FACE
    IN MY DEEPEST DARKEST
    HOLE-IEST PLACE

I WANNA WORSHIP YOU, JEEZ!
EAT YOUR BODY, DRINK YOUR BLOOD
FEEL YOUR WARMTH ALL OVER ME

OH WHIP ME JEEZUS!
NAIL ME, NAIL ME, TO YOUR CROSS

OH, PAPI JEEZUS
I'LL BE A BIG BRAVE MAN FOR YOU –

> (**JESÚS** *crouches down and playfully inserts the cross inside his body. It's awkward, funny and holy.*)

OH JEEEEEEEEEEEZUS!!
I WANNA BE YOUR LITTLE LAMB
BAAAA – BAAAAA

JOSÉ. Jesús!

JESÚS. Father!

JOSÉ. What are you doing?!

JESÚS. I swear that…

JOSÉ. Get dressed and put that back on the wall.

JESÚS. Dad…

JOSÉ. Get in the Car

JESÚS. I'm sorry, Father

JOSÉ. GET – IN – THE CAR!! We're going to church!

> (♫♫♫)

JESÚS. Everyone in Peru drives like a maniac, but Lieutenant José is especially in a hurry. Like the sin of putting the cross up my asshole is growing exponentially every minute.

JESÚS & JOSÉ.
WHOLLY HOLY HOLEY,
WE'RE GONNA SAVE YOUR SOUL NOW

JESÚS & JOSÉ.

>WHOLLY HOLY HOLEY,
>JEEZUS WILL MAKE YOU WHOLE
>
>WHOLLY HOLY HOLEY,

JOSÉ.

>MY SON IS NOT A FAGGOT!

JESÚS & JOSÉ.

>THE PRIEST, MYSELF AND JEEZUS
>WILL GUARANTEE THAT YOU WON'T TOUCH YOUR HOLE
>THE PRIEST, MYSELF AND JEEZUS
>WILL GUARANTEE THAT YOU WON'T TOUCH YOUR HOLE.

JESÚS.

The car screeches to a halt and Dad drags me inside the church. Splashes my face with holy water and shoves me inside the confession booth.

JESÚS & JOSÉ.

>NOOOO, NOOOO
>SHOULDN'T'VE TOUCHED MY HOLE
>NO, NO, NO, NOOO, NO, NO, NO, NO, NO!
>SHOULDN'T'VE TOUCHED MY HOLE

JESÚS.

>MY HOLE

CONFESSION

FATHER ANGELO. In the name of the Father, and of the Son, and of the Holy Spirit.

JESÚS. Forgive me, Father, for I have sinned. This is my first confession.

FATHER ANGELO. Go on, Jesús. You know you can tell me anything...

JESÚS. I... I stole Rosita's eraser.

FATHER ANGELO. Uh-huh... And... Have you been masturbating?

JESÚS. What?!

FATHER ANGELO. Who do you think of when you do it?

JESÚS. I... I...

FATHER ANGELO. Is your last chance to repent. It'd be a shame not to use it.

JESÚS. I... I...

MARÍA'S VOICE.
YOU ARE A MIRACLE...
YOU ARE MY MIRACLE, I'M HERE FOR YOU

JESÚS. I put a crucifix up my asshole, Father Angelo. And I was thinking of Jeezus while I was doing it – And I felt his love deep inside me! But I don't understand, Father! Should I be repenting for loving him or for not loving him enough? It's like I am condemned to suffer either way! Jeezus! Why have you forsaken me?

(**JEEZUS** *sniffs behind the curtain, unseen.*)

Father Angelo?

JEEZUS. You have to repent, Jesús. Is the only way Father can forgive us.

JESÚS. But why should I repent for feeling love? I love Jeezus and Jeezus loves me!

(**JEEZUS** *reveals himself.*)

JEEZUS. Yes he does!

JESÚS. Jeezus!

JEEZUS. Jesús!

JESÚS. Jeezus! I thought you were –

JEEZUS. It's always me behind the curtain, that's how it works.

JESÚS. Oh! Right... You came! After we –

JEEZUS. You HAVE to repent Jesús –

JEEZUS & JESÚS. Have you been working out?

JEEZUS. No! We can't! What we did in your room. Us! It's impossible.

JESÚS. I misunderstood everything, Jeezus! I thought you *loved-me* loved-me, I felt desire, I fell in love with you, I'm sorry! I –

JEEZUS. Jesús! I love-you love-you

JESÚS. You do? ...Then we can be together!

JEEZUS. Father will never permit it!

JESÚS. But... Aren't you and your Father like the same person?

JEEZUS. That's so silly, Jesús. Who told you that?

JESÚS. Then maybe we can speak to him! I know Fathers can be harsh at times but I'm sure he loves you very much.

JEEZUS. He sent me to Earth to kill me publicly...

JESÚS. Yeah, that is fucked up. I can help you, Jeezus.

JEEZUS. No... You can't...

EVERYONE WORSHIPS ME FOR MY SACRIFICE
DADDY PROMISED CRUCIFIXION WOULD SUFFICE
BUT HE KEEPS PIERCING MY FLESH WITH STEEL
CONDEMNS TO BE NAILED AND NEVER HEAL
SO ALL OF YOU CAN KNOW PARADISE

JESÚS.

YOUR BODY IS NOT SACRIFICE
WE DON'T HAVE TO COMPLY
WE DESERVE TO BE IN LOVE AND DEFY –

JEEZUS.

NO! FATHER'S POWER HOLDS ME LIKE A SPELL
AN ANGEL ONCE TRIED TO REBEL, AND WELL...
THEY FELL
ETERNAL FIRE BURNED THEIR SKIN
LOVE CAN BE A MORTAL SIN
IF WE KEEP GOING – YOU'LL BE SENT TO HELL

JESÚS.

IF LOVE IS A MORTAL SIN...
JEEZUS, I WONDERED
I PRAYED, YOU RESPONDED
OUR LOVE IS TRUE
I WILL BURN IN HELL FOR YOU

JEEZUS.

OH... FATHER WILL NEVER PERMIT IT

JESÚS.

NO! I AM A SINNER
I'LL EAT YOU FOR DINNER
WE'LL MAKE IT THROUGH
I WILL BURN IN HELL FOR YOU
HE SENT ME TO EARTH TO KILL ME PUBLICLY... BUT

JEEZUS & JESÚS.

WHAT WOULD I GIVE TO HAVE THIS STORY TO TELL
THE ONE IN WHICH A SINNER AND A GOD GET A ROOM IN
A HOTEL

JEEZUS & JESÚS.

TO WAKE UP IN EACH OTHERS LOVING ARMS
WANTING TO FUCK EACH OTHER IN THE BUM

IF LOVE IS A MORTAL SIN LET'S BURN IN HELL
IF LOVE IS A MORTAL SIN LET'S BURN IN HELL
IF LOVE IS A MORTAL SIN...

> *(They kiss. Seconds later an angry thunder scares them apart.)*

JEEZUS. But how? How?! Father's power is almighty! Tomorrow I will sacrifice my body and you will eat it –

JESÚS. I don't want you to suffer –

JEEZUS. We have to fulfill what's been written for us.

JESÚS. Let's run away!

JEEZUS. We shall be brothers!

JESÚS. No! Shut up Jeezus! That's fucked up! No!

JEEZUS. I'm sorry, Jesús. It's only my sacrifice that will save you!

JESÚS. I'm not the one who needs to be saved! If our love is a Mortal Sin, then it will stay inside of us forever.

JEEZUS. What do you mean?

JESÚS. Our fathers are obsessed with keeping us far from Sin, but it is a part of us! No one can take it away. Eating your flesh is not gonna save any– wait! That's it! Eat your flesh.

JEEZUS. That's what I'm saying!

JESÚS. No! I mean – I think I know how to save you, Jeezus... Let me show you!

> *(**JESÚS** starts praying to **JEEZUS** and telepathically explains the plan. **JEEZUS** reacts flustered.)*

JEEZUS. Oop! ...Woo! ....Jesús!...

> *(The prayer finishes and they look in complicity.)*

That *might* work. We can try...

JESÚS. Tomorrow, I swear I will save you –

JEEZUS. Oh my dad, oh my dad, oh my dad... It's my dad! You have to go now!

> *(**JEEZUS** casts **JESÚS** back to reality with his **JEEZUS** magic.)*

JESÚS. JEEZUS!! Jeezus?

FATHER ANGELO. So which is it? Have you been masturbating or not?

JESÚS. Oh, Father Angelo! Go to hell!

THE FIRST COMMUNION

(Sound effects – Ominous Organ Instrumental.)

MIGUEL. The whole family gathers in the front row of the chapel to witness Jesús' first communion.

Everyone is here: Mother María, Lieutenant José, All the aunties. Even Rosita is here still looking for her damn eraser..

All the boys in year six have been called upon one by one, walked to the pulpit in their camp white dresses and received the body of the Son of God. And finally the last name of the list is called.

Jesús walks towards the altar where Father Angelo is holding the last wafer in front of dead Jeezus. But instead of taking the wafer, Jesús turns around, faces the congregation and walks to the mic.

JESÚS. I... I... I would like to say something to my Father. Rosita, play the track!
  I KNOW I NEVER FIT YOUR EXPECTATION
  YOU TAUGHT ME LOVE WAS ONLY RULES AND PAIN
  WHEN YOU SAY "SACRIFICE" I HEAR "COLONIZATION"
  I SHOULDN'T BE THE ONE WHO BEARS THE SHAME

  SO YOU DON'T GET TO TELL ME WHAT FEELING LOVE IS
  TRUTH IS THE SEED INSIDE THE FRUIT FROM THE TREE
  THE POWER TO STOP HATRED AND INJUSTICE
  IS NOT COMING FROM HEAVEN, IS COMING FROM ME

  MORE POWERFUL THAN GOD
  WHAT ABOUT THE TRUTH MAKES YOU RAGE IN FEAR?
  MORE POWERFUL THAN GOD
  YES! I'M A SISSY! A FAGGOT! A QUEER!
  HOW CAN JEEZUS BE THIS HOT?
  IT WASN'T JUST A MIRACLE THAT BROUGHT ME HERE

MORE POWERFUL THAN GOD
LOVE IS MORE POWERFUL THAN GOD
I WON'T EAT THE BREAD, WON'T DRINK THE WINE
MY SOUL'S ALREADY PURE DIVINE
THIS TRUTH IS ALL I GOT
LOVE IS MORE POWERFUL THAN...
GOOOO-GOGHOOOD-HGOGOGOOHHGHG

> (**JESÚS** *blows life into* **JEEZUS** *by sexualizing a cross and performing "fellatio" to the image of Christ.* **JEEZUS** *materializes and is resurrected again as the music ends in a crescendo.*)

JEEZUS. It's the SECOND COMING!

RESURRECTION

GABRIEL. Jesús' Act of love made Jeezus resurrect again! In front of everyone at the Holy Trinity Academy Church School for Boys' Chapel

MIGUEL. And Jeezus came back to Earth! Free from his Father's orders as only a Mortal human being this time

GABRIEL. The structures of power in Catholicism were instantly dismantled.

MIGUEL. All the Vatican's money donated to end war, feed the hungry and fight for social justice.

GABRIEL. Jeezus and Jesús had to fix the relationship with their fathers.

MIGUEL. So they moved countries

GABRIEL. Traveled the world

MIGUEL. A settled down in the holiest place of all

MIGUEL & GABRIEL. South London

MIGUEL. Where they rent a one bedroom flat and celebrate their love.

GABRIEL. Jeezus convinced Jesús to write a musical

MIGUEL. Telling the story of a young boy,

GABRIEL. That learned how to be his own man

MIGUEL. By discovering the God he had inside...

GABRIEL.
> YOU ARE A MIRACLE
> YOU ARE MY MIRACLE
> I'M HERE FOR YOU

MIGUEL.
> In the name of my Father, and my Mother,
> And my holy self.

Our bodies in this room

Hallowed be our names,

Our queendom is earth,

Our will meaningless,

Anywhere and everywhere, all at once.

Let's share our bread daily

And forgive ourselves

As we forgive those who we love the most

Accept temptation

Fight evil

For this life, this godliness

This miracle is ours

Only until we die

MIGUEL & GABRIEL.

YOU ARE A MIRACLE
YOU ARE A MIRACLE
I'M HERE FOR YOU
IT'S BEEN ENOUGH WAITING
COME WITH ME AND LET'S GO
FIND OUR TRUTH

DON'T BE FOOLED BY SACRIFICE
OBEDIENCE, FLAGELATION
THE ONLY REAL HOPE OF SALVATION
LOVE... WHERE THE DIVINE TRULY LIES

YOU ARE A MIRACLE
YOU ARE A MIRACLE
I'M HERE FOR YOU
IT'S BEEN ENOUGH WAITING
COME WITH ME AND LET'S GO
FIND OUR TRUTH

(**MIGUEL** *and* **GABRIEL** *hold hands. A rainbow fills the sky.*)

(♫ **JEEZUS!** ♫)

www.ingramcontent.com/pod-product-compliance
Ingram Content Group UK Ltd.
Pitfield, Milton Keynes, MK11 3LW, UK
UKHW021551280725
461263UK00012B/115